D0585645

With

best wishes
and
warmest greetings
for Christmas

To

First published 1981 by
William Collins Sons & Co Ltd

© Pauline Flick 1981

This edition published 1990 by
Diamond Books, a division of
HarperCollins Publishers

All rights reserved. No part of this publication
may be reproduced or transmitted in any form or
by any means, electronic or mechanical, including
photocopying, recording or any information
storage and retrieval system now known to be
invented without permission in writing from
the publisher.

Flick, Pauline
Christmas cats
1. Christmas — Great Britain — History — 19th century
1. Title
394.2′68282′0941 GT4987

ISBN 0 00 215928 7

Designed by Trevor Vincent

Printed in Hong Kong

DIAMOND ♦ BOOKS

MAY YOU SPEND A MERRY CHRISTMASTIME.
Copyright.

Contents

INTRODUCTION

'When we sit "curtained, and closed, and warm" around the Christmas log-piled fire, incomplete indeed is our happy family circle if puss is not on the rug at its centre. Our playmate she has been from earliest childhood, and vainly may memory seek to recall the hour of our first introduction to the cat.'

MRS SURR – STORIES ABOUT CATS, 1882

The now familiar Christmas Cat, like so many pleasures of an English Christmas, seems to have developed into a national institution about the middle of the nineteenth century. Under the young Victoria, with her German consort and pretty children, everything combined to turn the old midwinter feast, with its robust amusements, into an altogether cosier and more sentimental domestic celebration centred on hearth and home. The special joys of a Victorian Christmas were all on an intimate scale suited to a family occasion, and soon every artist, printer, manufacturer and shopkeeper involved in the Christmas trade realized that the simple fireside cat perfectly conveyed the season's goodwill message, at least so far as its secular side went. For well over a hundred years cats of all shapes and sizes, often with bows and bells, sometimes in improbable suits of clothes, have adorned greeting cards and chocolate boxes, gazed from the top of bulging stockings or exploded out of spangled crackers; few of these inspired trifles were intended to be anything but ephemeral, but for all sorts of reasons many of them were treasured by long-forgotten lovers of cats, and against all the odds they have survived. Fragile links in a continuing Christmas tradition, these shabby playthings, worthless plum-pudding charms and faded calendars, still have a surprising power to touch the heart.

The wide variety of late Victorian Christmas Cats was born of a new regard for the animal world in general, and the feline race in particular. The superstitious cruelty of the Middle Ages and the casual acceptance, later, of the cat's usefulness simply as a catcher of vermin, gradually gave way to an appreciation of the little creature's finer points – its beauty, companionship, cleanliness and courage. Several distinguished individuals had already pointed the way: it was well-known, for example, that Sir Isaac Newton had ordered two round holes to be cut in his door, one for his cat and a smaller one for her kitten; that Dr Johnson had himself gone out to buy oysters for his poorly Hodge, fearful that the servants would resent being asked to minister to a mere cat; and that the Reverend Gilbert White had recorded the exceptional maternal instinct of a cat who had adopted and reared an orphaned leveret. From the middle of the nineteenth century, however, cats caught the popular imagination as never before, and a flood of pictures, stories, poems and news items both fostered and reflected the general enthusiasm.

One of the cat's foremost champions of this period was the artist Harrison Weir, who illustrated a huge number of animal books as well as writing manuals on cat care. In 1871 he organised the first of many Cat Shows at the Crystal Palace, and followed this up in 1887 by founding the National Cat Club, aimed not only at improving the various breeds but also at promoting the welfare of non-pedigree animals. In *Our Cats*, published in 1889, he combined practical advice with amusing anecdotes and tributes to his own beloved pets; he recalled his father telling him about the 'Happy Family' show that used to be set up on the Surrey side of Waterloo Bridge, consisting of a portable cage holding an assortment of animals, usually a monkey, an owl, some guinea pigs, squirrels, a magpie and a cat or two. On one occasion a burly spectator had conceded the wonder of small birds living happily with cats but had bet the showman that he could not keep mice with them; whereupon the showman lifted up one of the cats, triumphantly revealing a white rat and three white mice nestling comfortably underneath her. Weir

was at pains to emphasize that cats were also most useful animals, and that 'if there were not millions of cats there would be billions of vermin'; he particularly approved of official railway cats, singling out eight keen hunters kept at Trent Station to protect empty corn sacks; if only, he said, more cats had been employed in this way then some fine hams ordered by his uncle from Yorkshire would not have been completely devoured in transit by rats.

The breeding of pedigree cats became a fashionable pursuit, often involving expensive buildings and trained staff, and ladies in reduced circumstances were advised to take up this congenial employment. In 1888 the discovery of a cat cemetery at Beni Hasan, some hundred miles south of Cairo, stimulated fresh interest in the sacred cats of ancient Egypt: thousands of tiny mummified bodies were excavated, and although some found their way into museums the great majority, including a consignment shipped to Liverpool, were ignominiously turned into fertilizer. London dogs and cats, meanwhile, had a burial-ground set aside for them on the north side of Hyde Park, where many sad little headstones still stand, half-obscured by tall grass and wild flowers.

Christmas, however, was no time to dwell on the inevitable heartbreak of losing a pet, but a joyful occasion to be shared with frisky kittens and contented, purring cats. Sometimes, it is true, Christmas cats were used to point a moral, as was the case in a distressing poem published in 1882; too long to quote in full, the somewhat tedious verses describe a motherless boy called Johnny Ray, 'hungry and cold and friendless', who spends Christmas Day trudging through frosty streets looking for something to eat. He passes an open kitchen door

'And there on a mat
Was a sleek, gray cat,
In the warmth of a bright blaze, dining
Off fowl and fish,
On a piled-up dish –
Poor John! could he help repining?'

With the courage of despair he flies round to the front door, begging that he, like the cat, should be fed; though cruelly rebuffed by a footman the starving lad fortunately attracts the attention of the benevolent master, who immediately orders him to be brought in and given a meal. As might be expected in the 1880s, *noblesse oblige* goes even further and he is given a good job as well; all ends happily and John

Tall of his age,
Now a sprightly page
With a row of buttons shining
Opens the door
Where he knocked before,
At the cat's full meal repining.'

Books about cats were popular Christmas presents, and one of the most spectacular volumes of all time was *Henriette Ronner: the Painter of Cat Life*, published in 1891 and filled with pictures by the talented Dutch artist. A few years later Lady Chance produced *A Book of Cats*, a collection of her own lovely grey wash drawings backed up with reminiscences of her pets; these included the story of William, who went with her on a bicycle tour of the Wye valley, riding in a basket strapped to the handlebars. Edith Carrington's *The Cat – Her Place in Society* was published in 1896 by the Humanitarian League; the author tells how 'a poor little cat was found one day in Christmas week huddled against my door-step, beneath a blanket of snow'. Naturally the pathetic stray was taken in, and was soon confidently playing with the embroidered markers dangling from her benefactress's Bible. Edith Carrington's perfect description of stroking the little creature will surely find an echo in many memories:

'She is not satisfied till I have given her skull a gentle squeeze, eyes, ears, jaws and all, sufficiently strong to enable me to trace the whole of its anatomy. Then she bursts into a torrent of purring . . .'

An equally telling observation occurs in an elementary schoolboy's essay quoted in an 1890s magazine article entitled *Stray thoughts on Stray Cats*:

'The house-cat is a four-legged quadruped, the legs as usual being at the corners. It is what is sometimes called a tame animal, though it feeds on mice and birds of prey. Its colours are striped, tortusshell, black, also black and white, and others. When it is happy it does not bark but breathes through its nose instead of its mouth. Cats also mow, which you have all heard. Cats have nine liveses, but which is seldom wanted in this country because of Christianity. Cats eat meat and almost anything, speshully where you can't afford. This is all about cats.'

Nativity Cats

It would be unreasonable to claim anything but the frailest thread between the frolicsome Christmas tabbies of Victorian England and the sober cats accompanying the Virgin Mary in many paintings of the Italian Renaissance. All that can be said with certainty is that cats make excellent mothers, and are unfailingly attractive to human babies: for these reasons alone they must deserve a place in the general iconography of the feast of the Holy Birth.

There is no mention of cats anywhere in the Bible, although they were worshipped in Egypt and were so dear to Mahomet that he is said to have cut the sleeve off his coat rather than disturb a cat sleeping on it. It has been suggested that Old Testament writers could not bear to mention an animal sacred to their hated Egyptian overlords, and that even after Moses had led them out of captivity it would have been difficult for the nomadic Israelites to have kept cats or any other domestic pets. Despite this discouraging lack of documentary evidence, however, there are several legends connecting cats with biblical events, one of the best-known being the story of the cats in Noah's Ark: Noah, it seems, was worried about rats and mice eating his grain, and prayed for God's help; whereupon the lion sneezed, and out of its nostrils sprang two cats. The Italian artist Bassano never tired of painting scenes from the Flood, always giving the cat a prominent place in the procession in or out of the Ark, and in the romps on Mount Ararat. German woodcarvers invariably put a pair of striped or spotted cats – quite distinct from the larger lions, leopards and tigers – in the overcrowded toy Arks they supplied for the Christmas trade.

The belief that animals are able to speak on Christmas Eve is widespread, and so is the tradition that they kneel down at midnight, in adoration of the newborn Holy Babe. An Italian legend concerned more specifically with cats tells how a family of kittens was born in the Bethlehem stable on the first Christmas Eve, and these are usually said to have had crosses on their backs, like the Palm Sunday donkey. Perhaps there is a distant connection between these legendary Christmas kittens and the old Russian belief that a cat placed in the cradle of a newborn baby would drive away evil spirits, and bring good luck.

The traditional relationship between the Virgin Mary and a pet cat is more complex. Possibly it originated in a nebulous association of ideas linking the Holy Mother with Isis and Diana and their symbols of the moon and the cat. Alternatively the cat of Renaissance nativity paintings may have been intended as a portent of betrayal, as it was in representations of the Last Supper. To artists of the *Quattrocento* every animal and bird, every fruit and flower, had its esoteric meaning and it was usually no mere chance that led them to give the Baby cherries or corals or a red-splashed goldfinch to play with; these foretold the Passion just as the peacock symbolized immortality, the ox sacrifice and the ass humility.

Agnes Repplier, a great lover of cats and author of *The Fireside Sphinx*, suggested that the cat's homely simplicity served to highlight the spiritual significance of the miraculous events of the Annunciation and the Nativity. Writing in about 1900, she listed a remarkable number of cats in religious art, pointing out that St Ann seemed to have been as fond of cats as was her daughter and that, according to Italian tradition, several were present at the Virgin's own birth. Puccio's fresco in Orvieto Cathedral shows a white cat standing on its hind legs, trying to reach the food on St Ann's bedside table; at the Oratorio of S. Bernardino at Siena there is a black cat, while Luca Giordano placed St Ann's pet on the one and only bedroom chair and showed it sleeping peacefully on a cushion while everybody else is bustling round the new mother and her baby girl.

Cats present at the Annunciation are usually portrayed as placid creatures, quite unmoved by Gabriel's dramatic arrival. Even the riotous multitude of musical angels thronging the portico of the Hospital of S. Maria Nuova in Florence failed to disturb Taddeo Zucchero's drowsy pet. Frederico Barocci painted a fine grey cat asleep on the Virgin's work basket, and in another of his Annunciation pictures the cat reposes on a cushion. Only in Lorenzo Lotto's Annunciation at Recanati does a huge striped tabby flee in terror at the sight of the celestial messenger.

The young Leonardo da Vinci made a series of studies of the Holy Baby playing with cats. Dating from about 1478, there are versions in the British Museum, the Uffizi, and the Leon Bonnat Museum at Bayonne, although the finished work – if indeed it ever existed – has been lost. One of the British Museum drawings shows the Baby on his mother's knee, trying to hold a wildly struggling animal. In Barocci's *Madonna della Gatto* in the National Gallery the Holy Family has been joined by the infant St John, who is teasing a ginger-and-white cat by holding a goldfinch high above his head. Agnes Repplier mentions another Barocci Madonna with her lap full of kittens; presumably she had in mind the picture known as *La Vierge aux Chats*, showing members of the Holy Family clustered round the Virgin, who has a mother cat and kittens lying on her robe. There is a finished version of this painting in New York's Metropolitan Museum of Art.

There is, alas, no mention of cats in St Jerome's factual account, written in the fourth century, of the cave in Bethlehem where the Holy Family stayed, although he describes the very manger in which the Child lay, 'where the ox had known his Master and the ass the cradle of his Lord'. St Jerome is supposed to have kept a pet lion in his dwelling nearby, having gained its confidence by pulling a thorn out of its swollen paw, and Antonello da Messina was probably indulging in artistic licence when he painted the saint sitting in his study with a cat curled up at his feet.

Although St Jerome dismissed as nonsense many of the tales about Christ's childhood contained in the early Apocryphal Gospels, his contemporaries delighted in human stories of the ass that carried the Virgin to Bethlehem, or the ox St Joseph had brought to sell at the fair, the doubting midwives and the miraculous hay, and the equally miraculous bathwater. All these elements, together with sheep, camels, dogs, horses and other animals (which must surely sometimes have included cats) were later to have their place in the elaborate crêche scenes set up first in Rome and Naples and which were to become an essential part of Christmas all over the Christian world.

The strangest of all explicit references to nativity cats, however, comes not from Bethlehem or even from Rome, but from Edwardian England. In 1904 the Reverend Gideon Ouseley published *The Gospel of the Holy Twelve*, a work which he believed had been communicated to him, in dreams, by four departed mystics. These included Emmanuel Swedenborg (d.1772), the Swedish seer, and Anna Kingsford (d.1888), a well-known animal lover who had been received into the Catholic church by Cardinal Manning. Ouseley claimed that the Gospel – now almost entirely

forgotten – had been translated from an early Christian document preserved in a Buddhist monastery in Tibet, where it had been hidden by the Essenes. The account of the Nativity is a mixture of familiar verses from the Authorized Version interspersed with material from Mr Ouseley's dreams and visions, and the passage of the greatest interest to cat-lovers reads:

'And there were in the same cave an ox, and a horse, and an ass, and a sheep, and beneath the manger was a cat with her little ones, and there were doves also, overhead, and each had its mate after its kind, the male with the female.

'Thus it came to pass that he was born in the midst of the animals which, through the redemption of man from ignorance and selfishness, he came to redeem from their sufferings . . .'

Further on there are alleged accounts of Christ rebuking some youths for tormenting a cat, and later of his befriending a little stray which he hands over to the care of a widow named Lorenza. In the Introduction to his extraordinary work Ouseley reminds his readers that the cat and the dove were 'specially honoured and protected in Egypt (most ancient centre of civilization, religion and philosophy and true science) as the symbols of Isis, the foreshadower of the "Divine Mother" of Christianity.' Whatever one may think of the reliability of the source material, *The Gospel of the Holy Twelve* is a most interesting period piece, illustrating contemporary preoccupations with spiritualism, animal welfare, Egyptology and even freemasonry. It is only fair to record, also, that the Reverend Gideon Ouseley was co-author of another book, this time a straightforward treatise on *How to Keep a Cat in Health.*

Christmas Card and Calendar Cats

'The most casual observer cannot have failed to remark the wonderful development in late years in "Catty" Christmas souvenirs, thus giving proof of the growth of love and admiration for pussy. We have cat almanacks, cat calendars and cat annuals and I can testify to the innumerable Christmas cards with designs of all sorts and conditions which have found their way into my hands.'

FRANCES SIMPSON – A BOOK OF CATS, 1902

Cats must outnumber any other animal that has ever appeared on a Christmas card; robins, asses and oxen run them close, but no other creature has quite the same gift for conveying a cheery greeting, or can be treated in so many engaging ways. Generations of designers have worked out endless variations on the basic feline theme, producing merry cats entangled with paper decorations, reaching up into Christmas trees, eating plum puddings and carrying sprigs of holly; black cats bring New Year luck as well.

The first Christmas card – without any cats, it must be admitted – appeared in 1843, and during the next forty years or so a vast industry developed, supplying cards to suit all tastes. The firm of Raphael Tuck began producing Christmas cards in 1871, and Kate Greenaway's association with the card department of Marcus Ward dates from the same year. A decade later – here cat lovers prick up their ears – Louis Wain sold his first card designs and made enough money to rent a room he could use as a studio.

Probably these early Wain designs were based on birds and 'conventional' animals, as the archetypal Louis Wain comic cat does not seem to have arrived until the late 1880s. This is not to say that there was any shortage of amusing cats before this – indeed, cards from the early 1880s include some of the most diverting Christmas kittens ever produced. The majority of them were printed in Bavaria by means of exquisite chromolithography (a technique of making multi-colour lithographs by using a different stone or plate for each colour of ink), although the designs were by British artists and featured roly-poly native cats quite unlike the thin, cross-looking felines portrayed by most continental illustrators. Some very attractive double-sided cards seem to have been particularly popular for cat subjects: published by Hildesheimer & Faulkner, they cleverly combined both back and front view of

some little tableau such as a group of cats climbing up a barrel, or a family of kittens breaking into a toy drum; another depicted the back and front of a large tabby head, which opened up to reveal a collection of cat drawings and a greeting by that prolific versifier, F. E. Weatherly.

By 1899 Raphael Tuck was doing such a huge trade in 'Christmas cards, calendars, books, engravings and a thousand and one other forms of beautiful decoration' that the company moved into splendid purpose-built premises in London's Moorfields. Three of their calendars were reproduced in Frances Simpson's *Book of Cats* to illustrate the enormous popularity of feline ephemera; these cut-out cardboard decorations featured fluffy cats swinging on a clock pendulum, sitting in a basket and balancing on a pair of scales. By a lucky chance the full range of calendars produced in 1896 by another Anglo-German firm, Ernest Nister, has been preserved in the British Library. A bulky volume made up of trade samples in mint condition reveals page after page of assorted almanacks printed in full colour, with dozens of tiny 'purse' and 'pocket' calendars ornamented with cats and other animals. One large calendar shows a feline version of the Royal Academy on Opening Day, which at first glance suggests the hand of Louis Wain, although there is no signature. However, careful comparison with signed drawings in various children's books published by Nister, and with some original water-colours in the Victoria and Albert Museum, indicate that it is more likely to be by William Foster, son of the celebrated Myles Birket Foster. As well as conventional farmyard animals and birds William often drew comic dressed-up cats, and at times his work is all but indistinguishable from Louis Wain's.

Louis Wain.

It is, however, Louis Wain's cats that have become inseparably bound up with our Christmas festivities; 'Christmas without one of Louis Wain's clever catty pictures,' observed Frances Simpson, 'would be like a Christmas pudding without the currants.' For years *The Illustrated London News* and *The Illustrated Sporting and Dramatic* included major examples of Wain's drawings in their special Christmas supplements, and seasonal set pieces like *A Cats' Christmas Dance* (containing over a hundred and twenty cats and kittens) were eagerly collected. In 1896 Roy Crompton wrote a touching tribute after meeting Louis Wain and his favourite cat, Peter; by now 'Peter the Great' was getting old, and Roy Crompton explained that he felt *'inclined to wake him up and whisper how, one cold winter's night, I met a party of five little children, hatless and bootless, hurrying along from an East-end slum, and encouragingly saying to the youngest, who was crying from cold and hunger, "Come along, we'll get there soon." I followed them some distance down the lighted street, till they paused in front of a barber's shop, and I heard their voices change to a shout of merriment, for in the window was a crumpled Christmas supplement, and Peter, in frolicsome mood, was represented entertaining at a large cats' tea-party. Hunger, cold and misery were all dispelled. Who would not be a cat of Louis Wain's capable of creating ten minutes' sunshine in a childish heart?'*

Years afterwards there was a sad postscript. In the late 1920s, as a chronic mental patient in Bethlem Royal Hospital, Louis Wain was invited to help with the Christmas decorations; going up to a large, wooden-framed mirror, he painted on it a scene of gleeful cats sitting round a plum pudding. Afterwards the unique mirror was carefully stored away, to be brought out again each year as part of the ward's decorations, and it still survives at the present Bethlem Hospital in Beckenham.

A different type of comic cat was produced by the American photographer Harry Whittier Frees (1879–1953) whose animal studies involved real kittens and puppies wearing clothes. Frees had an extraordinary talent for persuading his little sitters to pose in the most unnatural ways, and it was claimed that absolutely no coercion was ever used.

Postcards featuring his animals – in particular Rags, the star cat performer – were extremely popular from 1905 until about 1960, being reproduced by various firms all over the world. Many were over-printed with a simple Christmas greeting, and some incorporated a tiny bellows mechanism so that the cats could be made to squeak.

Nursery Cats

A, B, C,
Le chat est allé
Dans la neige; en retournant
Il avait les souliers tous blancs'

The French version of 'A, B, C, Tumbledown D' conjures up a pretty picture of a Christmas cat in the snow; coming to the last line, the mother lifts up the baby's feet in their white knitted shoes, just like the cat's snowy paws. Nursery rhyme cats are among a child's first favourites, and of course a real-life kitten, properly treated, makes a perfect playmate; Kipling recognized this when he made the Cat that Walked by Himself earn a place in the humans' cave by amusing the baby.

Celluloid, horribly inflammable and all too easily dented, was nevertheless widely used in toy manufacture; early in the 1900s a tiny cat's head, hardly bigger than a cherry, was beautifully moulded in this material by the German Rheinishe Gummi firm.

But real kittens are generally in short supply in December (early summer is the season for desperate, heart-rending advertisements for loving homes) and in any case they should never be regarded as mere playthings. Responsible present-givers are wise to choose appropriate toys or books to satisfy the longing for a Christmas cat.

A cat of the usual soft toy variety is in fact notoriously difficult to make, great skill being needed to capture the delicate contours of the head; often a stuffed cat looks more like a teddy bear. Despite this problem toy manufacturers have managed to produce hordes of different cats and kittens for the Christmas market, ranging from expensive fur-covered automata to cheap little cardboard figures.

Cat ninepins were popular about the turn of the century; they were made of felt or plush and firmly stuffed with wood shavings, and then mounted on turned wooden bases. A full set comprised eight grey animals clad only in neck ribbons and bells, and a splendid king-pin in a sequinned red coat and a crown.

LITTLE KITTENS
TIDLEY WINK
2
4
1
5

At the same period the talented German toymaker Margaret Steiff was designing stuffed fur-fabric animals of unprecedented quality, and her influence is still discernible in the natural-looking soft toys of today.

Printed paper was the basic ingredient of many playthings of the late nineteenth and early twentieth centuries. During this golden age of toys the same Bavarian factories that supplied the Christmas card trade produced innumerable coloured pictures used in the making of building blocks, sand-toys, games, doll-dressing sets, pop-up books and scrap motifs; the subtle effects these firms achieved by chromolithography and embossing techniques have never been surpassed. Cats were prominently featured: for example, one elaborate set of picture cubes could produce cat noises at the tug of a string, and Raphael Tuck included a delightful cat with several changes of costume among their paper dolls; 'movable' books were full of cat pictures that sprang to life, and sand-toys displayed performing kittens that operated in magical, jerky silence.

Christmas pantomime cats are especially dear to children, and no production of *Puss in Boots* or *Dick Whittington* would be complete without the feline star taking a stroll round the auditorium and shaking paws with his admirers.

Both stories go back for hundreds of years (*Dick Whittington* being based on fourteenth-century fact) and countless versions appeared in early children's books; as pantomime cats they made their debut in the 1880s, when Augustus Harris took over the management of the Theatre Royal, Drury Lane, and introduced the spectacular dramas that were to become an essential part of the Christmas holiday.

Puss presents a Rabbit to the King

At the Giant's Castle.

Happily Wedded.
RAPHAEL TUCK & SONS LTD. LONDON, PARIS & NEW YORK
No 905
Designed in England
Printed in Germany

A 'Hush' motto was ornamented with a monkey feeding a cat, and when the lantern became overheated, or the audience too excited, 'An Interval' could be declared by either 'Cats nursing kittens' or 'A Kitten Pie' (no further explanation given, unfortunately).

Less heady entertainment was provided by the Magic Lantern, which remained popular until well into the twentieth century. A box of new slides made a splendid Christmas present, and *Dick Whittington* and *Puss in Boots* were among the favourite sets. A tantalising assortment of subjects is listed in the 1907 Army and Navy Stores catalogue, including single 'motto' slides designed to punctuate the main attractions. A performance could be heralded by a slide reading 'With the Season's Greetings' – described as 'very funny and seasonable, two cats in a hamper with their heads over the side of the basket'.

Cotton cats with fur and features simply printed on the cloth, sewn up like tea-cosies or cushions, can be surprisingly life-like. This type of cat toy seems to have been pioneered by the Arnold Print Works of North Adams, Massachusetts, who patented a design for a mother tabby and two kittens in 1892; in England Dean's Rag Book Co. Ltd. (famous for soft toys as well as indestructible books) had great success with similar cotton cats which they called 'Fluffikits'.

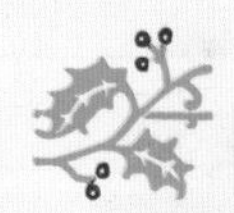

CATS AT THE CHRISTMAS FEAST

Sometimes, as a further refinement of pleasure, between the courses of a protracted feast, a basketful of kittens would be brought in, each guest choosing one from this furry bouquet, to fondle before the next course was announced, and the little creatures superseded by some pilaff scented with pomegranates.'

LESLEY BLANCH – PAVILIONS OF THE HEART, 1974

This Persian custom, enchanting though possibly not very hygienic, would never have found widespread favour at an English Christmas dinner. 'Put Kitty down, dear, you don't know where she's been' – the chilly nursery refrain reverberates too strongly in the Anglo-Saxon subconscious for many real cats to be allowed to share the festive board. Even so, our Christmas meals have several less controversial feline associations, both edible and ornamental.

Harrison Weir recalled seeing gingerbread *Puss in Boots* figures sold at fairs, as well as 'cats made of cheese, sweet sponge cake, sugar' – once he had even seen a cat made of jelly.

Gingerbread moulds in cat shapes were certainly known in the eighteenth century, and Edward Pinto, who built up the wonderful assortment of wooden bygones now in Birmingham's City Museum, examined the moulds in his collection and fell to wondering exactly how they were used; with characteristic thoroughness he and his wife experimented with various recipes and came to the conclusion that if the gingerbread mixture was to hold its shape it would have to be made according to a seventeenth-century recipe, the main ingredient being breadcrumbs; the mixture was never baked, but pre-cooked by boiling before receiving the impression of the mould.

The cliché of the chocolate box cat was coined in 1868 when Richard Cadbury had the brilliant idea of adding a picture to a box of chocolate creams – then an expensive luxury – and so turning it into an attractive gift. His portrait of his daughter, 'a blue-eyed maiden, some six summers old . . . nursing a cat', was the picture chosen, and thus the young Miss Cadbury's pet became the first of a long line of winsome tabbies to act as powerful sales-aids to confectionery manufacturers. By the 1870s biscuits were being specially packed for the Christmas trade; the Reading tinsmiths Huntley, Boorne & Stevens (associated with Huntley & Palmer since the 1830s) produced a huge range of fancy containers shaped like handbags, Moorish tables, kitchen stoves, perambulators and scores of other unlikely objects; pictures of domestic pets were unfailingly successful, and a scene of dogs and cats enjoying a party together was particularly suitable for the season of peace, goodwill and merriment.

Tiny silver cats, with other good luck charms, threepenny bits and miniature china dolls, used to be hidden in plum puddings.

The tradition probably had its roots in the French custom of concealing a silver trinket or a white china 'bean' in the *Gateau des Rois* served on Twelfth Night; whoever found the trinket became King of the Feast. The following day three slices of cake, ostensibly kept back for the Holy Family, would be given to the poor.

Sweets actually shaped like cats are always in demand, either to put in stockings or to hang on the tree. And the nearest approach we have to the exotic bouquet of live Persian kittens seems to be a basket of three little cats, all made of chocolate and wrapped in coloured foil, far too engaging ever to be eaten.

The most usual ornaments for the top of a Christmas cake are rotund Santa Clauses and eskimo babies in gritty snowsuits, but small china

cats have also been made for this purpose. German manufacturers had the monopoly of supplying these minute, unglazed ceramic figures, and trade catalogues of the 1920s and 1930s show an astonishing variety. Cats are not very easy to find, but one little ornament took the form of a jolly black kitten posting a Christmas card in a red pillar box and another was modelled on a marmalade cat sitting beside a small basket which served as a candle holder.

Christmas crackers, too, have cat associations; colourful cat 'scraps' have often decorated the outside of crackers, while the contents used to include sleek little cats made of black glass with flashing 'diamond' eyes. Tens of thousands must have been imported from Bohemia over the years; after exploding from their exquisite wrappings they were usually carried off to grace over-furnished dolls' houses, where a considerable number still reside.

CHRISTMAS FOR CATS

'Christmas Tree For Cats. – *I read somewhere – in Lord Broughton's Memoirs, I think – of an old lady who prepared a Christmas tree for her cats. It was hung with herrings, and they walked round it solemnly before being presented with the special delights it supplied. They must have been well trained not to spring up and detach the fish.*'

Letter to NOTES & QUERIES, 31st December, 1938

Although Lord Broughton's *Recollections* have been searched, the source of this charming story has not yet come to light. Bearing in mind that Christmas trees were rarities in England before about 1850, readers might like to indulge in a seasonal parlour game and put forward suggestions as to whose memoirs might have included this fishy reminiscence.

Like the old lady with the herrings, most cat-lovers do arrange special treats for their pets at Christmas, some going so far as to buy pre-packed stockings filled with delicacies and toys. But few 'private' cats can have celebrations to compare with those enjoyed by Paddington Station's famous Tiddles: picked up in 1970 as a tiny stray, Tiddles was given a home in the Ladies' Cloakroom on Platform No 1, soon growing to an enormous size and becoming an object of wonder to every (female) traveller descending into his subterranean domain. From Advent Sunday until Twelfth Night the spirit of Christmas illuminates this unlikely grotto as Tiddles holds court, his giant basket festooned with tinsel and shining ornaments. Mrs Watson, his devoted attendant, provides him with a lighted Christmas tree and arranges the cards sent by his admirers all over the world. The effect is magical; tired women, at first reluctant to believe their eyes, smile with delight and give cries of joy. Children stroke him, and their mothers make donations towards his food fund. They all go on their ways looking cheered, as if touched by some unlooked-for Christmas blessing.

I have to end these Christmas gleanings on a personal note. First, because as I was putting them together a small Christmas cat decided to take up residence with me; he had been found wandering the streets, wearing a red collar and obviously tame, but all efforts to trace his owner had failed. I meant to take him down to our cat sanctuary, but had to keep him in London for a few days first. One night he refused to come in when called at bedtime, preferring to cavort about on some nearby scaffolding. In the end he had to be left outside with a makeshift box prepared for him in a shed. The next morning I came downstairs to find the sitting room carpet covered with soot, and Jack – as he was afterwards named – curled up as usual on a pale blue chair. Admittedly he could have climbed onto the roof easily enough, but how he had known which of eight possible chimney pots led to his favourite couch remains a mystery. I can only say that his descent took place in mid-December, just a few days after the feast of St Nicholas.

Finally, I would like to dedicate these pages to the many friends who have helped the Rollright Stones Cat Sanctuary, either by giving a home to a needy kitten or by generously contributing towards the cost of feeding the rescued strays who live there permanently. Visitors coming to see a prehistoric Stone Circle must often be taken aback to find a tribe of happy cats gambolling among the ancient megaliths, but almost always surprise gives way to concern, and the interest complete strangers show in these little animals is very heartening.

Acknowledgement

The author would like to thank the following for their help in the preparation of this book:

Mrs June Astle-Fletcher for permission to photograph *The Cats' Christmas Dance*;
Mr S. B. Ross of Cadbury/Schweppes for the photograph of the chocolate box;
Miss Caroline Dudley of Brighton Museum for the gingerbread mould;
Mr Ronald Clark for the two small cats on the front endpaper,
the card facing Contents and the cats' Christmas cracker card;
Miss Sue Read of Reading Museum for permission to use the Huntley and Palmer biscuit tin;
Mr Don Nicholson for the photograph of the tin and the Louis Wain drawing;
Mr Mark Byford for the word puzzle;
Miss Sylvia Willgoss of Dean's Rag Book Co. Ltd. for the 'Fluffikits' photograph;
and Mr Rodney Dale for information about Louis Wain.

The Ernest Nister calendar is reproduced by permission of the British Library;
the Leonardo da Vinci drawings by permission of the Trustees of the British Museum;
and Barocci's *Madonna della Gatto* by permission of the National Gallery, London.
Back endpaper: Dick Whittington magic lantern slides, c.1900.

1

2

3

7

8

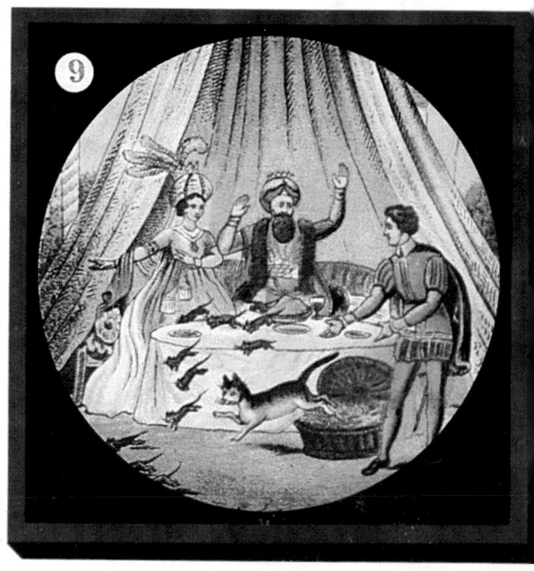
9